Roger Zahab

Collected duos for violin and cello

scores

Roger Zahab | Collected duos for violin and cello

contents

notes on the music   iv

Sonata for Winter   6

Passencore Double   14

grata per i tuoi suoni   26

the young person's guide to convergence   36

notes on the music

In gathering these duos from key moments in my life I have finally understood how important the combination has been to me as a musician. The Kodaly Duo, op. 7 was the first chamber work I struggled to play at around age 17. The Ravel Duo was critical in my understanding of how carefully chosen ideas can grow organically into a large form, and the Brahms Double Concerto, finally, taught me very important lessons in humility. As a violinist in equal partnership with a cellist, it was also the place I learned how essential it is to watch out and care for one's partner as much as one's self: flaws cannot be hidden, but attention to the other's intonation, rhythm and sound can yield such intricate beauty and tonal variety gratefully remembered years later and somehow informing all my other adventures.

rz july 19, 2020

Sonata for Winter, completed December 10, 1979, was written for Betsy Highland, a gifted cellist and fellow graduate student at SUNY Stony Brook - I think she asked for a duo we could play together. This is perhaps the first work in which I was able to keep an ear on matters large and small, and I took particular care to consciously write in audible phrases (which may have been daring for the time: I seem to recall that clearly audible phrases - and also octaves and triadic sonorities creating any sort of harmonic gravitational pull - were frowned upon as "not advanced". But then, composers considered me a violinist and violinists considered me a composer - perhaps things haven't changed all that much.) As with most works from my turbulent youth, there is a hidden quote from a Romantic era composer.

It was premiered by us on April 2, 1980 on a Mostly From the Last Decade concert in Staller Arts Center, Stony Brook, New York. rz

Passencore Double was written mostly during spring and early summer of 1993 and is inscribed to the composer and cellist James P. Hinkley.

The word "passencore" comes from the first page of James Joyce's Finnegans Wake, something about Sir Tristram, a "violer d'amores... had passencore rearrived from North Armorica..." with double meanings from the French: pas encore - not yet, or passe encore - still going on, continuing. The title becomes a password to my duplicitous compositional technique and to those who journey to destinations near and far.

David Russell and I gave the first performance in Akron, Ohio on September 7th, 1994, and George Faddoul recorded us in Ravenna, Ohio, on May 19, 1995.

grata per i tuoi suoni, which can be translated as "*grateful for your sounds,*" was written for Eric Gratta, who for four years ardently and thoughtfully supported so much musical activity at the University of Pittsburgh and beyond.

While it is perhaps my most classically balanced form it is also a palimpsest of superimposed life experiences and sonic memories which change even as they surface and are heard. Underneath all these interwoven lines is the timeless chase of sea and shore, and the knowledge that turbulence resolves into calm. Meaning and emotion are discarded like objects abandoned to be pounded and dissolved by the sea into grains of sand until no memory, no evidence is left behind - only the sound of waves caressing the shore. rz

The first performance was given by Eric Gratta, cello and Roger Zahab, violin on March 26, 2016 at Chatham University, Pittsburgh, Pennsylvania.

the young person's guide to convergence was written for David Russell and shares some material with another violin/cello duo, grata per i tuoi suoni, written a month or so earlier. Here the materials revolve around each other in continuous variation, the balances shifting without the extremes of my earlier work - perhaps an equilibrium has been found. After David and I gave its first performance on October 5, 2019 on A Roger Zahab Portrait concert presented by Music on the Edge at the University of Pittsburgh in Bellefield Hall Auditorium, I felt compelled to "revision" it and now present it here in the final version. rz

Sonata for Winter
for violin and cello

for Betsy Highland

Roger Zahab
(1979)

© copyright by Roger Zahab BMI All rights reserved corrected May 24 2016

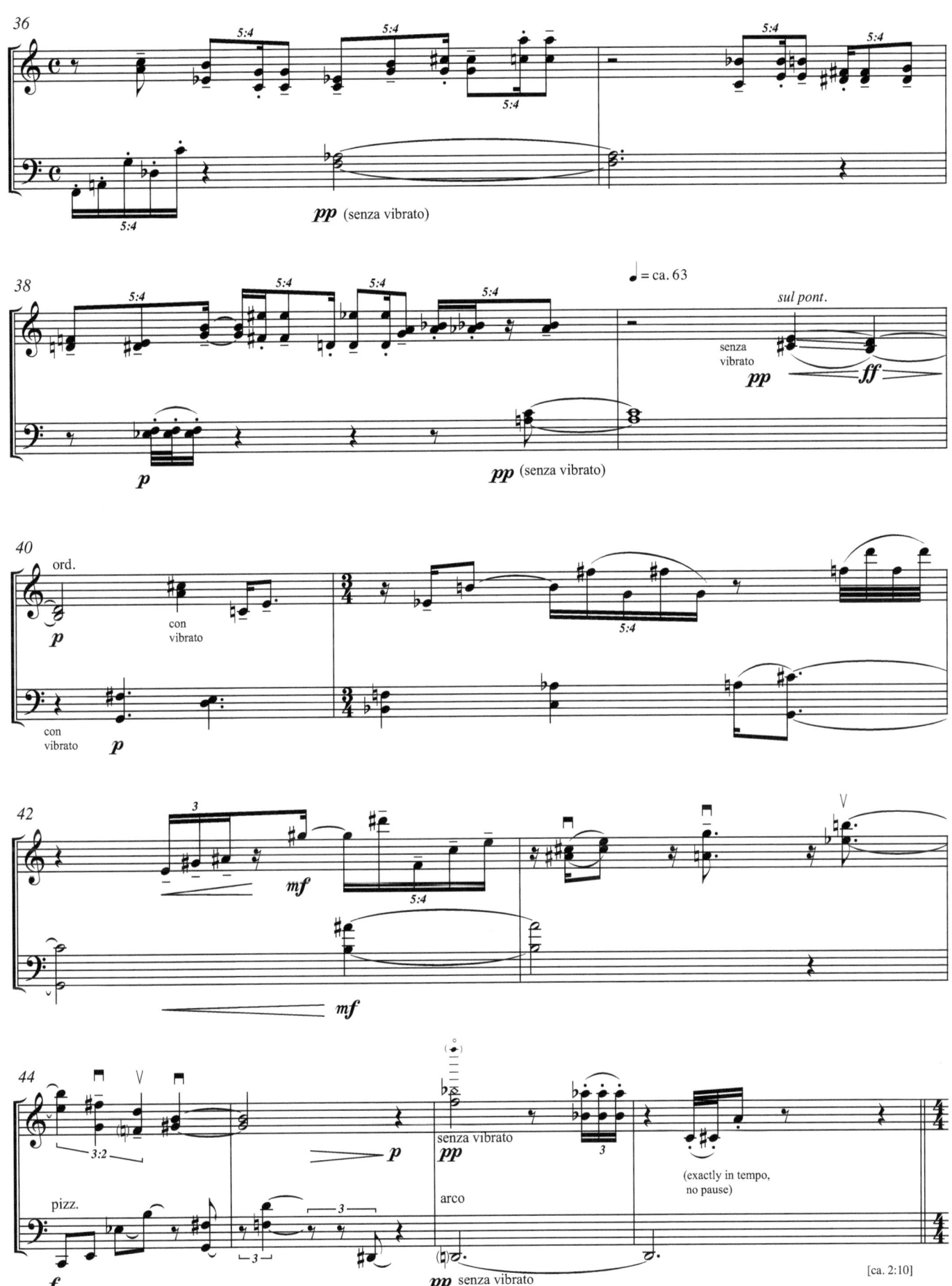

[1:30]
duration about 7 min.

10 nov.-10 dec. 1979
Setauket, NY

to James P. Hinkley

Passencore Double

Roger Zahab
(1993)

© copyright 1993 by Roger Zahab BMI All rights reserved

edited july 18, 2020
corrected

Zahab Collected duos for violin and cello — Passencore Double

Bare and serene

ca. 3 min.

10. May 1993 - Akron, Ohio

Passencore Double

Harbor dance

18 (fold out 5a)   Passencore Double   Zahab Collected duos for violin and cello

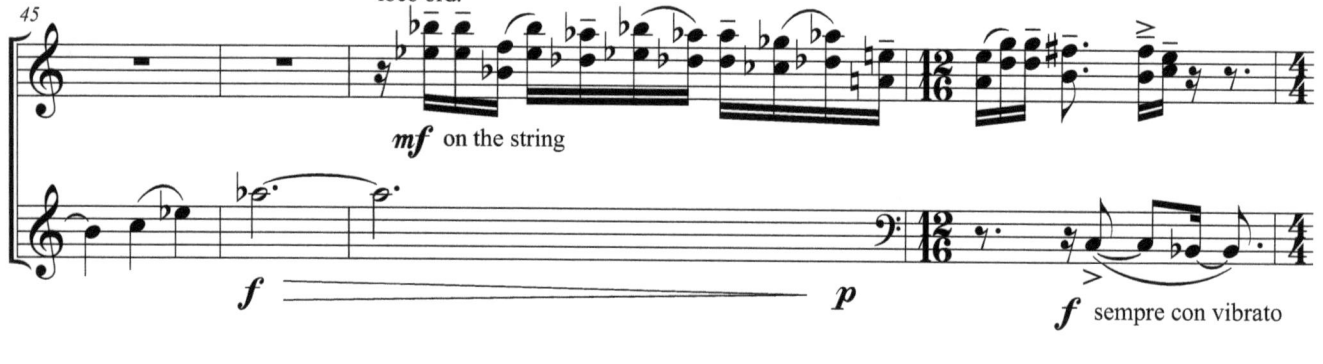

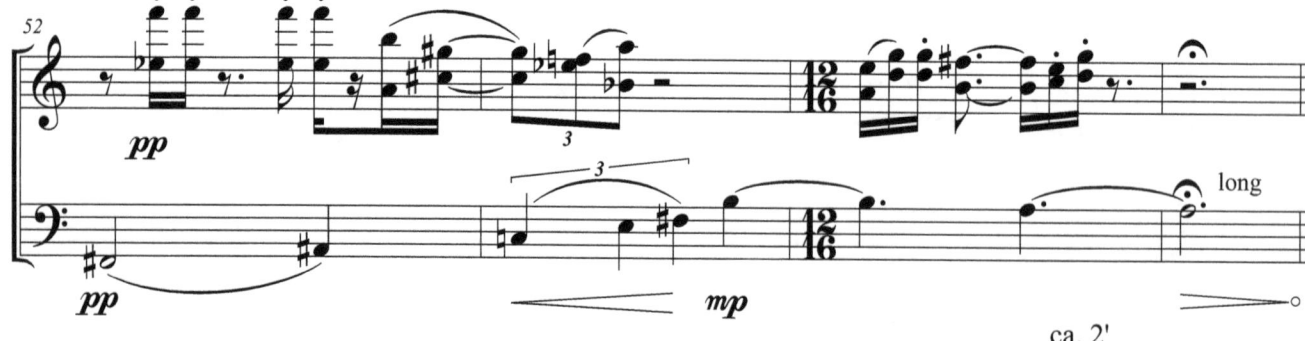

ca. 2'
24. May, Little Rock, Arkansas

Passencore Double

brief pause

ca. 3'
27-30 May
Little Rock, Arkansas

... and of Desire

Passencore Double

Feb. '89, Akron/ 2. June '93 Little Rock ca. 4 1/2 min.

Departures/Arrivals

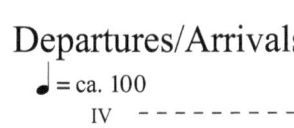

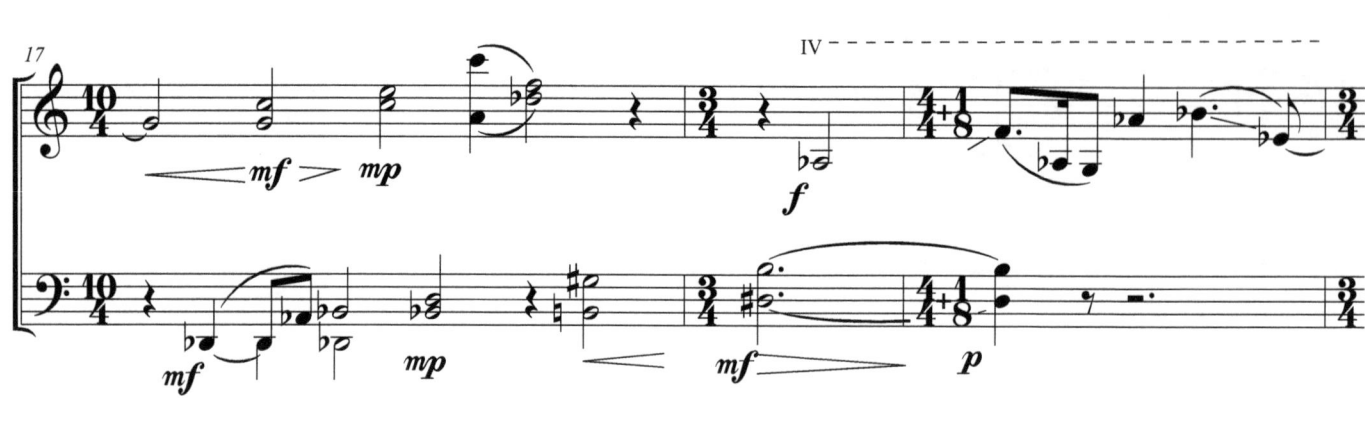

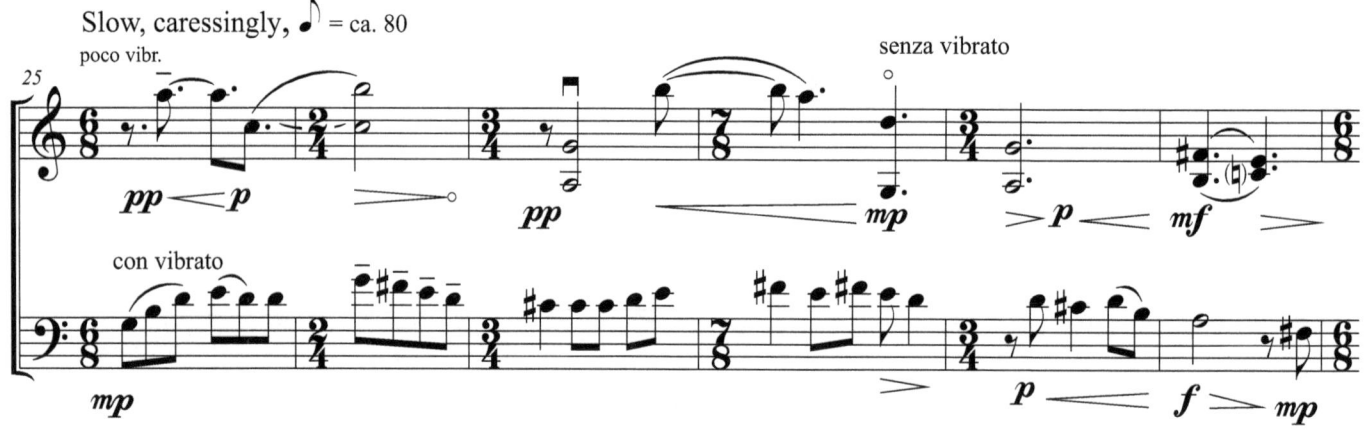
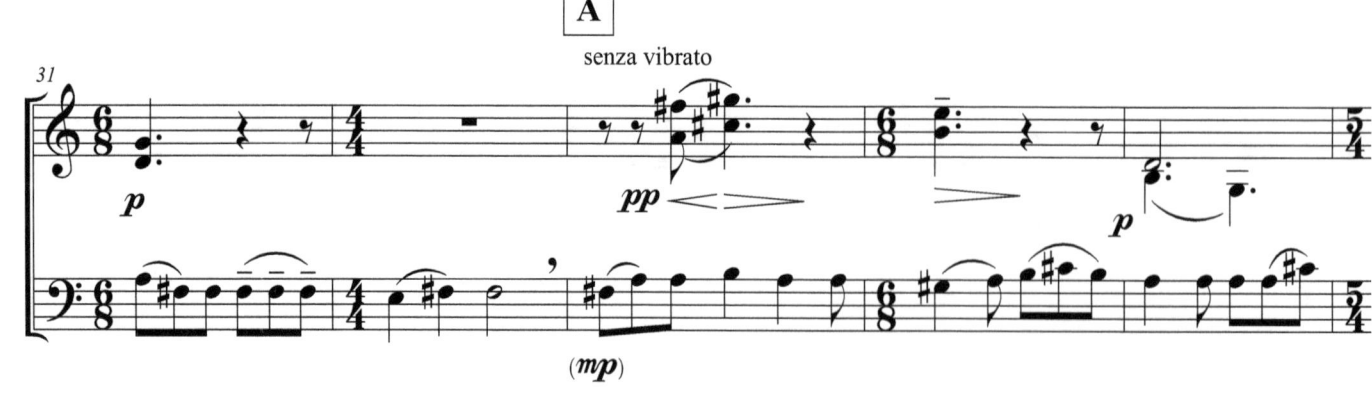

Zahab Collected duos for violin and cello Passencore Double (fold out 11a) 25

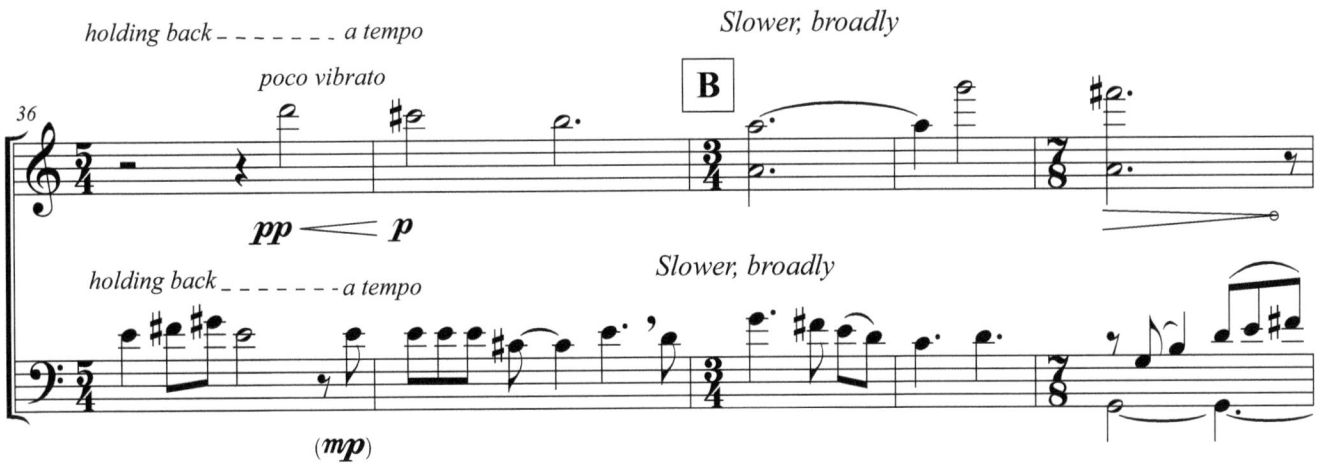

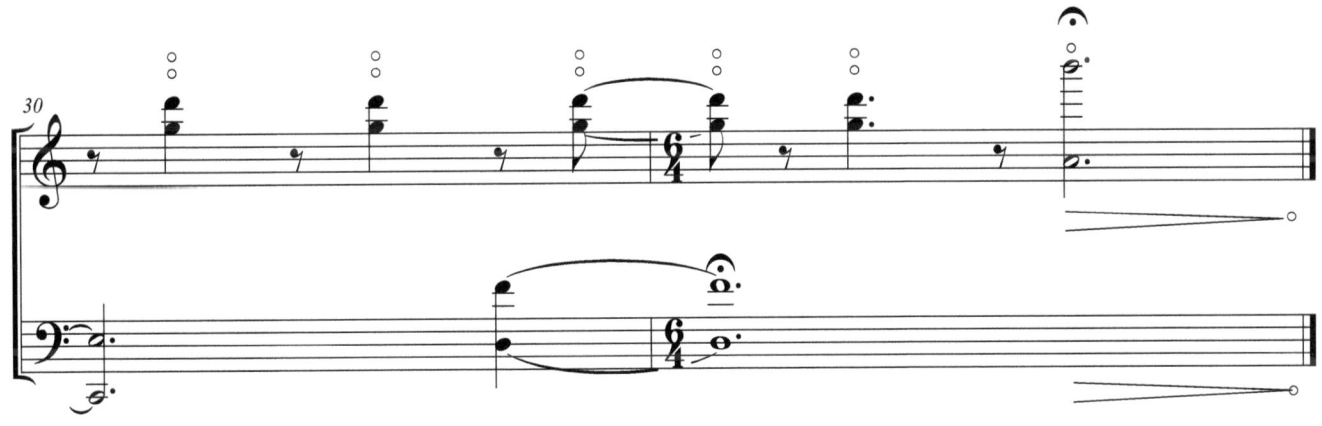

ca. 3 1/2 min.

17. Dec. 92
7. Jan - 16. June 1993
Akron - Little Rock

total duration about 16 minutes

for Eric Gratta

grata per i tuoi suoni
for violin and cello

Roger Zahab
(2015)

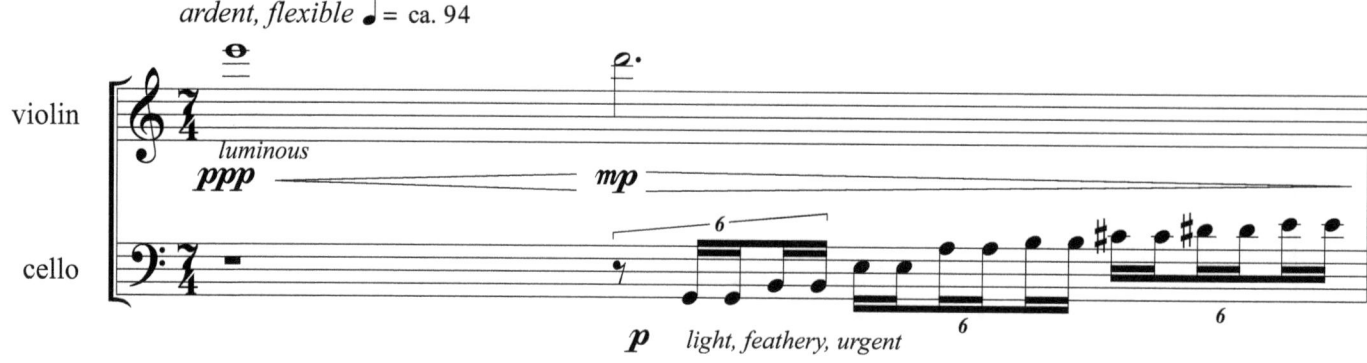

© copyright 2015 by Roger Zahab BMI All rights reserved

grata per i tuoi suoni

Zahab Collected duos for violin and cello — *grata per i tuoi suoni*

grata per i tuoi suoni

grata per i tuoi suoni

Zahab Collected duos for violin and cello — *grata per i tuoi suoni*

Zahab Collected duos for violin and cello *grata per i tuoi suoni* 35

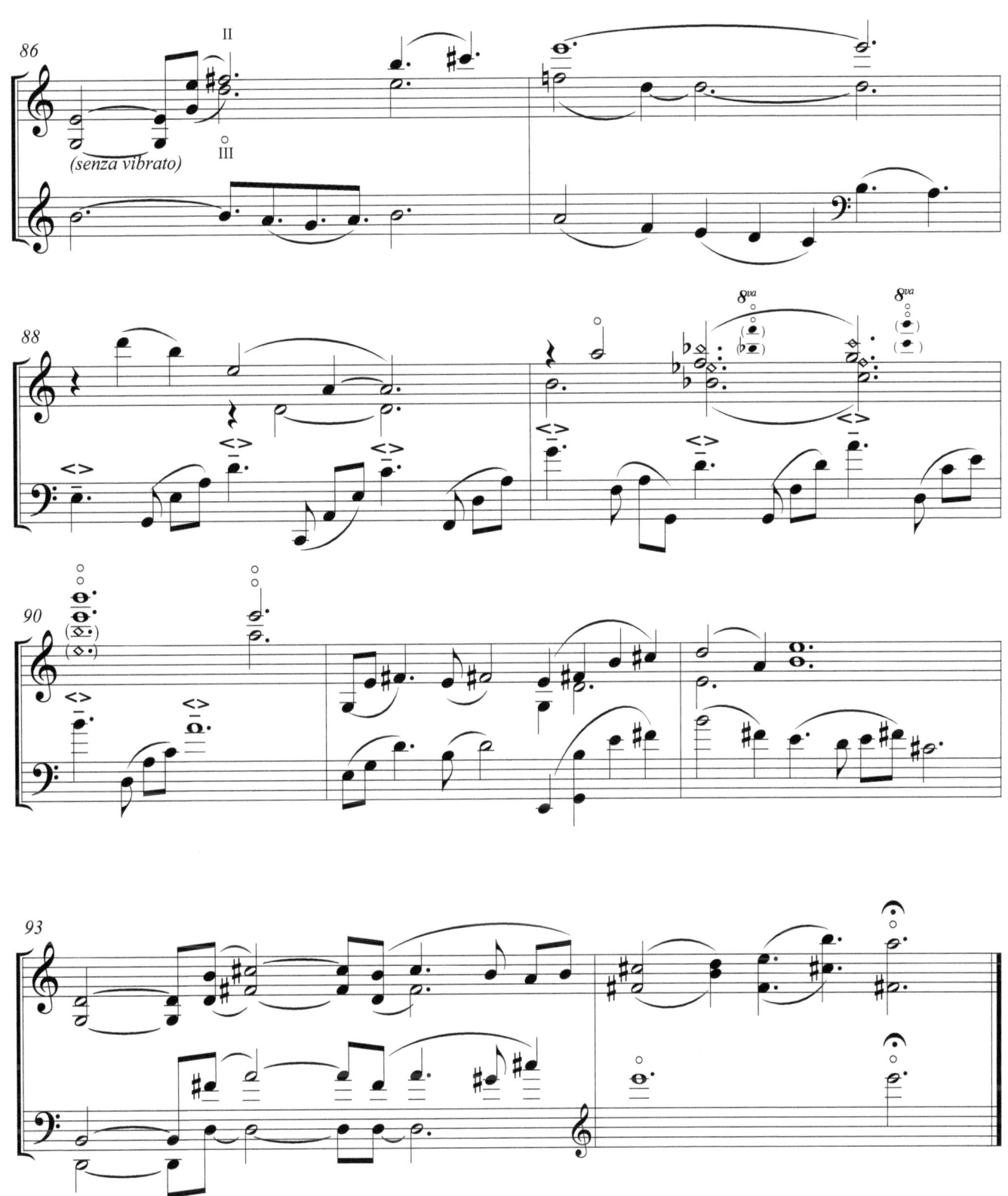

october 28-november 20, 2015
Pittsburgh
about 8 minutes

44 — the young person's guide to convergence

Milton Keynes UK
Ingram Content Group UK Ltd.
UKHW051948100424
440928UK00010B/219